Hamsters as a Hobby

G. Ovechka

SAVE-OUR-PLANET SERIES

Contents

987654321 **1996 Edition** 95 789

Distributed in the UNITED STATES to the Pet Trade by T.F.H. Publications, Inc., One T.F.H. Plaza, Neptune City, NJ 07753; distributed in the UNITED STATES to the Bookstore and Library Trade by National Book Network, Inc. 4720 Boston Way, Lanham MD 20706; in CANADA to the Pet Trade by H & L Pet Supplies Inc., 27 Kingston Crescent, Kitchener, Ontario N2B 2T6; Rolf C. Hagen Ltd., 3225 Sartelon Street, Montreal 382 Quebec; in CANADA to the Book Trade by Vanwell Publishing Ltd., 1 Northrup Crescent, St. Catharines, Ontario L2M 6P5; in ENGLAND by T.F.H. Publications, PO Box 15, Waterlooville PO7 6BQ; in AUSTRALIA AND THE SOUTH PACIFIC by T.F.H. (Australia), Pty. Ltd., Box 149, Brookvale 2100 N.S.W., Australia; in NEW ZEALAND by Brooklands Aquarium Ltd. 5 McGiven Drive, New Plymouth, RD1 New Zealand; in Japan by T.F.H. Publications, Japan—Jiro Tsuda, 10-12-3 Ohjidai, Sakura, Chiba 285, Japan; in SOUTH AFRICA by Lopis (Pty) Ltd., P.O. Box 39127, Booysens, 2016, Johannesburg, South Africa. Published by T.F.H. Publications, Inc.

MANUFACTURED IN THE UNITED STATES OF AMERICA
BY T.F.H. PUBLICATIONS, INC.

With time and patience, most hamsters can be hand tamed. Photo by Michael Gilroy.

INTRODUCTION

A cinnamon hamster investigates the gustatory possibilities of a lemon wedge. Photo by Michael Gilroy.

Each person chooses a pet for different reasons. Some animals are chosen for the companionship that they provide, some for convenience, some for status (like expensive purebreds), and some because they are adorable. Some animals are chosen for a variety of these reasons, and the hamster is one of them. Hamsters are easy to care for. They can be kept in a small apartment; they don't create any kind of disturbance or make any kind of mess. They are adorable and cuddly and cute. They can provide lots of entertainment and they are responsive. Hamsters really don't require much from their owners. They need a good-sized cage placed in a suitable location where there is enough ventilation and not too much light. They are not very expensive to purchase or keep. They just need a lot of love and attention from a responsible owner.

Hamsters do a lot of interesting and amusing things—one of which is the way they hoard food in their cheek pouches. The hamster, whose name comes from the German word *hamstern* which means "to hoard," stuffs food into his pouches until he looks like a baseball player with a chaw of chewin' tobacco, or a trumpet player practicing his musical art. And after he has filled his cheek pouches—which stretch and expand—up like a balloon, he scurries away to hide his booty—often underneath his mattress of natural wood shavings.

Hamsters like to play, usually in the evening or night, because they are nocturnal creatures who often sleep the day away burrowed in the sleeping area of their cages. Some hamster owners, in fact, have filled entire rooms in their homes with hamster toys, setting up for the hamster an elaborate playground made of exercise wheels, slides, ladders, even rides and other sources of amusement— for both the hamster and the hamster owner.

If hamsters are treated kindly and given a comfortable, roomy cage that is kept clean, they are gentle and responsive pets. And as any pet owner knows, you get from a pet what you give to that pet.

To begin with, one thing this means is that you should not simply put a hamster in a cage and forget about it. If you're at all interested in this animal—and, presumably, that's why you decided to get a hamster in the first place—you'll want to try, in a sense, to make friends with it.

That means handling them. Hamsters like to be handled. They like to play, and they like you to play with them. After a while, they start to recognize your voice and will even sit up on their hind legs and listen when you talk to them—especially if you just happen to have a tasty hamster treat in your hand. One hamster owner says that her hamster listens for her to come home at night and then sits on her lap and watches TV with her!

You may also like the hamster because of the interesting variety of colored coats that it sports. Originally introduced to the pet scene and to pet lovers as the golden or Syrian hamster, this little animal has been bred since then in countless other colors. Today, there are white or albino hamsters, black hamsters, panda hamsters, Teddy Bear hamsters and many other color variations. Chinese and dwarf hamsters, from other regions of the world, are also available and popular as pets today.

Hamsters are energetic and inquisitive creatures that respond immediately to toys of any description. These animals definitely appreciate diversions! Photo by Michael Gilroy.

SELECTING A HAMSTER

Because so many different types of hamster have been bred, and because these come in all shapes and sizes and colors and because all are different, it would not be a good idea to

walk into the first pet store that you see and take just any hamster. Look around. One good way to start: find out if any of your friends or if any of their friends have hamsters. Go to their homes and see the

Hamster toys should be rugged enough to withstand considerable activity! Photo by Michael Gilroy.

animal in action, and see if this is the kind of pet you would really like to take home.

Then again, it has also been said that one reason why people have animals is to learn about life from

While there are certainly no iron-clad rules, it has been suggested that hamsters really make better pets for the older child—those nine years old and up, for example. One reason for this might be owing to the hamster's short life span. Hamsters normally live about 1000 days. It has been suggested, and observed in some cases, that younger children might not be able to deal with the passing of a pet. A younger child, of about five or six years of age, might, it has been suggested, get attached to his pet and not be able to fully understand or accept the death of that pet.

them. And what better way could a child learn about the facts of life *and* death than by this kind of experience? But this decision—at what age the child should have a hamster—should be left up to parents and guardians. Whatever the age, though, the hamster owner should be a responsible guardian of his or her pets, one willing to accept the responsibilities, such as feeding and cleaning the cage, that go along with the fun of pet ownership.

So, you've decided to get a hamster. You've been to one pet store to look at the

Despite the numerous strains and color varieties today, the Syrian, or golden, hamster remains both the most popular and familiar type on the market. Photo by Michael Gilroy.

stock and you've seen the Syrian, or golden, hamsters. Then you've been to the pet store down the road where they also have the all-white or albino hamster with his pink eyes. Someone mentioned that there is a black hamster, and you definitely want to see one or two of them before you decide which

hamster, with his brown or ruby eyes—and which, at times, looks like a stuffed animal. You can also get a panda hamster, which is spotted brown or beige on a white coat.

What about the long-haired Teddy Bear hamster which also sports different-colored coats? Or how about a dwarf hamster, two kinds of which—the Chinese striped hamster and striped, hairy-footed dwarf

you want to take home with you. But don't stop here: there are other color varieties— all springing from the original golden hamster—to choose from. There's the cream-colored

Longhaired hamsters require greater attention to cage cleanliness and coat care. Photo by Michael Gilroy.

hamster—can be found in more and more pet stores?

Meanwhile, as your search goes on for the right hamster, you may want to look up someone from the local 4-H Club because this organization may have members who raise hamsters and might be able to give you helpful advice about selection.

The worst thing that you can do is to make a hasty decision. Hamsters don't just appear from out of nowhere. There is always the possibility that a hamster may be ill-tempered because it has been treated badly in its early life or because it has been shipped improperly, with only a few scraps of food and water in a cold crate.

This leads to other important factors involved in selecting a hamster. You'll want to make sure that the one you bring home is in good physical condition and has a good, even disposition. You absolutely do not want to get an animal that has been suffering from a case of "wet tail," a most definite sign of poor health.

If you're seriously considering a certain hamster, ask the person in the pet store to take it out of its cage and put the animal on a counter or table where you can get a better look at it. Don't try to take the animal out of the cage yourself, but watch how the person showing it to you does it. It says a lot about the pet store if the people who work there are comfortable when they are handling animals. They should also know a lot about animals and be able to answer your questions to your satisfaction. It also says a lot about the pet store—and your chances of getting a good pet there—if the people who work there seem to be interested in and seem to *care* about pets.

After the hamster you like—golden, white, black, beige, panda, dwarf or Teddy Bear—has been placed on the counter or a table in the pet store, do not reach for him right away. Always give an animal time to adjust to things, especially if he is taken out of his environment.

A good way to make friends with a hamster is by offering him one of the many treats and snacks the pet store will probably have. Hamsters *do* bite, and it *does* hurt, so be very careful. When the little animal seems to be warming up to you, extend your hand...slowly...and offer him a hamster pellet or a hamster "veggie." Do this slowly and smoothly because he is still going to be a little nervous.

While all of this is going on, look the hamster over. You want one who has some weight to him, who looks solid. You don't want one that is too skinny or bony. The fur should be soft and thick (but not on a Teddy Bear

hamster). The hamster's eyes should be clear and the animal should look alert.

You want a young hamster. How young? About five or six weeks old. Don't forget about the hamster's shorter life span. If you get a younger animal, you'll be able to have him longer. And you'll also be getting a pet that will be easier to tame and train. The pet store owner or helper will be able to tell you the correct age of the hamster.

You *don't* want an animal who shows any signs of having wet tail. You don't want one whose fur is ruffled or gooey. You don't want to see any scars or bald patches in the hamster's fur. You don't want a hamster that looks lethargic, whose movements are slow. Its eyes should not be runny, nor should the nose. And look at the anal area—make sure it's dry.

There may be tiny "breeders' marks," and there may be small spots on the hips which feel thicker than the rest of the hamster's skin. These pigment spots are normal. Other lumps, tumors, and bumps or forms of disfiguration are not normal.

A male or a female? The general consensus is that male hamsters have a better reputation for being more gentle and good-tempered. Female hamsters, especially during the breeding cycle, can be natural killers—of their mate, and, in several instances, of their young. If you get a "couple," you'll also need separate cages. While the male hamster is normally less driven to this kind of aggression, even he, at one point in the breeding cycle (when the litter has been delivered), can kill the young. While things are generally quite tense all around during the breeding cycle, under other

A healthy hamster is bright eyed, alert, and interested in his surroundings. Photo by Michael Gilroy.

This Russian hamster presents a very different appearance from the much more commonly kept golden hamster, which originated in Syria. Photo by Susan C. Miller.

conditions two males can share a cage. It is not advisable for a female hamster to have a roommate.

If you decide to get a female hamster—and they are a little bigger and heavier than the males— make sure that she is not pregnant. The folks who are helping you in the pet store must be able to determine this for you. If the female is pregnant, it will mean a lot more work for you, not to mention the addition of probably around seven other hamsters to take care of. If the female is about to deliver a litter, the condition will be fairly obvious, but a less prominent bulge may escape the casual eye.

How many hamsters do you want? If you do want to breed them, understand that they are very prolific breeders, capable of delivering a litter of, say, eight in 16 days, and they can breed all over again shortly after that. If you are going to breed hamsters, please do not take this casually. It's a lot of work, and it means finding homes for many other hamsters.

If you want just one hamster for starters, there is no need to worry that he or she will be lonely living by himself or herself. If the pet is taken care of properly, given a comfortable, roomy cage and proper attention, he or she will be happy living alone.

While cost is certainly a factor in selecting some other animals, hamsters are not expensive at all. Cost is minimal, and you shouldn't even be thinking about it in terms of selecting a hamster...unless, of course, a price quoted is way out of line with what others are asking. What you *should* be thinking about, in addition to the color and type of hamster you want, is the physical condition of the animal.

A young male Golden hamster. Photo by Michael Gilroy.

GETTING EVERYTHING READY

Experienced pet owners know just how important it is to be organized when it comes to taking care of animals. Things will always go a lot more smoothly if you already have everything you need for your new hamster in your home before you bring him home.

So, let's go shopping for your new hamster. What will your shopping list look like? You'll need, above all else, a cage or a tank with a good supply of wood shavings or chips for the hamster's sleeping and very important piece of physical fitness equipment for the hamster. There, that should do it... No, wait a minute, better get a gnawing stick for him to chew on!

Now that you have

toilet areas. A water bottle, which can be attached to the cage, is also very important. A sturdy food dish which the hamster, who gnaws and chews on everything, won't be able to upset in the cage is another good thing to have ready. Have a good supply of hamster pellets, which can easily be purchased from your local pet shop dealer. While you're out shopping for your new animal's arrival, it might also be a good idea to have the hamster's exercise wheel ready. It's not just a toy; it's also a everything ready at home for the hamster, and now that you have brought the new addition into your house for the first time, there's just one other thing to remember: allow him to get used to his new surroundings gradually. It would be best to give the animal the cage and food and water and then leave him alone for a while. Any animal is going to be nervous in a new environment — especially if people are all grabbing him, picking him up and putting him down. The atmosphere for a new pet

Pet shops carry a wide variety of housing units designed especially for hamsters. Some of these housing units come equipped with cage fixtures such as exercise wheels and food bowls. Photo courtesy Rolf C. Hagen Corp.

should be on the tranquil side. He might be frightened by loud noises, such as slamming doors, loud music or TV, or a lot of people hovering over

Be sure to offer your hamster ample quarters to both alleviate boredom and foster cleanliness. Photo by Michael Gilroy.

biggest cage that you can afford. The hamster is a very active little creature who likes to do all kinds of him.

Put the hamster's cage in a cozy corner of the room that is not too warm and not too cold and where there is not too much light. Let him get used to the place and in a day or two you can gradually start to get to know him a little better—until you reach a point where the hamster feels at home in his cage and with you.

THE RIGHT CAGE

Hamster cages *can* be considered "adequate" by some if they measure 12 inches by 12 inches by 12 inches in height. But this is really too small. It would be wise to get a larger, roomier cage, one that is about 24 inches in length, 18 inches from front to back, and about 12 inches from the bottom of the cage to the top.

You may find cages that are even bigger. Get the

acrobatic tricks. You should, in fact, encourage him to stay active and get this kind of exercise. A hamster that has been kept in a cage that is too small and which doesn't enable him to get the right amount of exercise can get nervous and snappish.

Bird cages and fish tanks have been used as hamster housing. Whether you decide on a commercially manufactured hamster cage or a bird cage or a fish tank, you must always make sure that enough air circulates. In fact, one argument against use of the tank for the hamster is the possibility of a certain amount of humidity build-up. A hamster's surroundings should always be kept dry—and clean, of course. The tank, it has been said, traps some of the hamster's own

Pelleted food formulated especially for hamsters is the main part of a hamster's diet. Photo courtesy of Rolf C. Hagen Corp.

body heat, which in turn generates a certain amount of humidity, especially if the air circulation in the tank is not good. Some tanks do provide adequate ventilation and may be used. A 10 gallon tank is a good-sized hamster home.

Cages should also be easy for you, as the hamster's principal housekeeper, to handle. Many commercially manufactured cages are streamlined for easy handling, which is fine as long as they are sturdy enough to withstand the lifestyle of the hamster and the frequent house cleanings for which you will be responsible. Some hamster owners have purchased commercially made hamster cages only to find that the cages they bought were too flimsy—pieces of the cage would

snap and break under the slightest pressure. It's always a good idea to go with a product that looks and feels a little on the sturdy side. In addition to your frequent cleanings of the cage, that cage is also going to be gnawed on and chewed on by the hamster.

Most cages today are made of plastic and metal, preferable for a number of reasons. One is that hamsters will gnaw wood, which activity might fill the cage—and the hamster's sensitive cheek pouches—with splinters.

Plastic and metal are also preferred to wood because wood absorbs urine and will create dampness in the cage. Certain cages are equipped with sliding trays, made of plastic, glass or metal, to make it easier for you to clean.

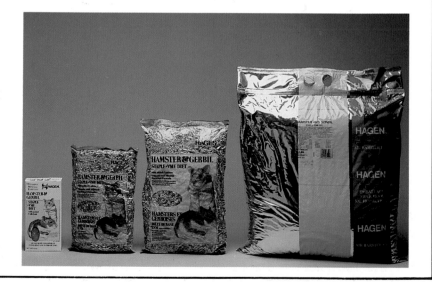

The "roof" or top of the hamster's cage, whether it's a specially-designed hamster cage, tank or bird cage, should be secure and escape-proof. Hamsters are always looking for ways to get out of their cage and they know how to do it. Make sure the top of the comfort in mind. The cage should be deeply padded with wood shavings or wood chips. Natural cedar or pine chips should be spread out over the bottom surface of the cage to a depth of one to two inches. Hamsters sleep and hoard food in one area of their

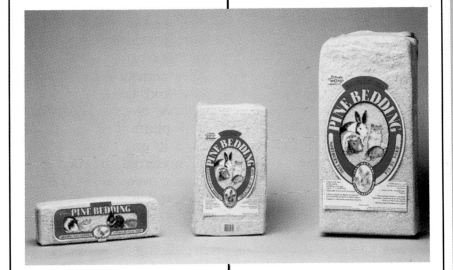

You can choose from a wide variety of materials with which to line the cage bottom. Be sure to provide a deeper layer in your pet's sleeping area. Photo courtesy Rolf C. Hagen Corp.

cage and any other openings in the cage are secure.

While the cage roof can be made of wire—so the hamster can climb up the swing on the bars—the bottom of the cage shouldn't have a wire or wire grating surface.

In addition, while the hamster's cage should be sturdily constructed of plastic, metal and wire (no wood) the interior of the cage should be furnished with the hamster's need for

cage, using these materials. And they use these same materials in another part of their cage for their toilet.

Use extra layers in the sleeping area; the hamster, who likes to burrow, will appreciate that. Don't, however, put pieces of cotton or old blankets or towels into the cage. The hamster will chew on them and probably ingest bits and pieces of cloth.

In addition to a weighted food dish, the hamster's

cage should have a water bottle attached to it. Don't use a water dish, which may become contaminated or knocked over by the animal. A bottle helps keep things clean and dry in the cage. Most can be attached to the cage. Make sure the inhabitant is able to reach it to get water. If the spout is too high the hamster might not be able to reach it. Always check water levels to make sure that the water bottle is working properly. It is a good idea to provide a fresh supply of clean drinking water every day.

The hamster's housing, whether it's a cage or a tank, should be placed in a location where it's not too bright and where it's not too drafty. Don't put the

hamster's cage directly in the sunlight. Don't put the cage near a window or on the floor. The best place for it is in some cozy corner of the room on a table or a stand.

Hamsters like temperatures that are a little on the warm side, preferably in the 65° to 72°F (18–22°C) range. If, however, you like things a little cooler, you should take extra steps to make the hamster's living area warmer. One way to do this is to keep the storm windows in the room closed. You might also provide the hamster's cage with a little more insulation and warmth by putting a blanket over it (remembering the need

Golden hamsters interacting and "getting away from it all." Photos by Michael Gilroy.

to maintain good air circulation) or by adding an extra layer of insulation underneath the hamster's cage. You can also close the heating vents in your room or your side of the room while keeping them open in the hamster's room or the hamster's side of the room. In the summer or warm weather, keep your pet away from the air conditioner or air conditioning vents.

Don't let the temperature in your house drop below 15°F (13°C). Hamsters can come down with a kind of winter numbness, caused by this drop in temperature. It goes into a state of hibernation, which more than one hamster owner has confused with rigor itself. In hibernation, the cold hamster will sleep, the body gets rigid and the animal's body temperature drops as well. If this situation does develop, you can thaw out the hamster by first of all

turning up the heat, and secondly by warming him up gently with your hands.

The hamster's sensitivity to cold and to sunlight (its eyes weren't designed for exposure to bright light) are two reasons why the cage should be generously filled with wood shavings. If it gets too bright or too cold, the animal can always burrow deeper in the cage where it is darker and warmer.

In hibernation, or asleep? This particular hamster was asleep to the degree that it could be lifted from its cage without waking it! Photo by Michael Gilroy.

A HAMSTER'S PLAYGROUND

One reason why people like hamsters is the fact that they are entertaining little fellows who like to play. You can bring out his natural playfulness, and also help to satisfy his need for important exercise, by setting up a hamster playground.

The hamster playground can be as elaborate as you like, but every one should include an exercise wheel. It's fun for the hamster to run on; he will use it, and it will provide a good way for him to get the right amount of exercise that he needs. This need for exercise can't be emphasized enough. Without enough of it, the animal can fall victim to a form of cage paralysis.

The habitrail™, available in most pet stores, is kind of a combination playground and amusement park for hamsters. You can start with some of the basics and keep adding on, similar to adding new pieces to an electric train system. There are "Whirl-A-Wheel" rides for the hamster, "Sky Pet Houses," "Sky Spinners," and "Speedstreak Racers."

There are also ladders, slides, revolving wheels and stairways to upper floors for the hamster to climb. Remember one thing, though: the more intricate and the more interesting some of this may be, the more diffi- cult it will be to clean and to keep clean.

While the hamster will use these toys, don't force him to. He should play because he wants to

An occupied hamster is a happy hamster. Toys, in fact, can be considered essential cage fixtures as they contribute to your pet's well-being. Photo courtesy Rolf C. Hagen Corp.

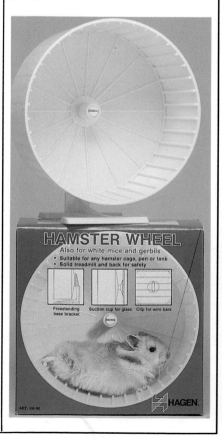

play, not because you want him to.

The commercial manufacturers of hamster equipment have certainly covered most of the bases when it comes to the hamster playground. But those who are handy or who like to provide the homemade touch can also use books, pipes, tubes and other props found around the home to create still other diversions for their pets. Hamsters like to play in and hide in mazes and caves. You can also fill up a "sandbox" of wood shavings for them to burrow in, hide and sleep.

If you do choose to become a junior carpenter and construct some home made hamster toys or hide-

A longhaired hamster chomps on a carrot while perched on its "playground." Photo by Michael Gilroy.

This mature hamster has the look of a miniature teddy bear! Photo by Michael Gilroy.

a-ways, be sure that everything you put into the cage is secure and won't come tumbling down. Make sure tunnels are wide and ladders won't fall. If you use heavier materials to create little nooks and crannies, make sure that these materials, such as bricks or heavier pieces of wood, can't topple over.

WHAT TO FEED A HAMSTER

What do you feed a hamster? As is the case with people, there is no "perfect" diet; dieticians and nutritionists, not to mention the average person, all have their own pet theories about what kind of food one should or shouldn't eat. So don't be surprised to hear the same differences of opinion when it comes to feeding animals.

Of course, everyone will agree that a hamster, like any other animal, needs a well-balanced diet with the right amount of vitamins, minerals and other nutrients. Today, most of the makers of commercially prepared hamster food have developed products that contain most everything a hamster needs to stay healthy and active. Available in most pet stores, these nutritious dry food pellets should form the basis of its diet for this and two other important reasons: they are easy to hoard; and gnawing on the pellets helps keep the hamster's ever-growing teeth from growing too long.

Everyone will also agree that variety in the hamster's diet is important. One simple way to start developing some variety in it is to serve

By nature, hamsters are seed eaters, but as with all creatures, variety is the spice of life! Photo by Michael Gilroy.

your pet hamster pellets and basic hamster chow from the different pet food makers' product lines. Try different brands from time to time.

Now here is where you, as a pet owner, might go in a different direction than another pet owner. Pet owners have different ways to supplement their animals' diets. One basic difference is in the "home made versus store-bought" approach to shopping and feeding. Just as the commercial pet food chefs and nutritionists have found the right formula to create food products that provide balanced nutrition and the basic part of the hamster's diet, so have they also been able to develop an entire line of hamster treats, snacks and other food supple-ments.

On the other hand, you can provide this kind of food supplement yourself, in large part by going to your local health food store. You might be surprised to learn that a lot of food your hamster likes can be found there. And you'll also discover that what's good for you may also be good for your hamster. Hamsters eat rolled oats, buckwheat, filberts, peanuts (a very good source of the important vitamin E requirement), sunflower seeds, corn, and wheat germ. They also like a little cereal once in a while, and a bit of dry bread. Of course, just as tastes vary with people, hamsters' tastes will probably vary too.

Some hamsters might like certain foods more than others.

So it depends on how you, the pet owner, want to serve these food supplements. If you like the idea of getting something that's already made, you will be able to choose from a wide variety of commercially prepared hamster snacks and treats. Hamsters, it might be added, will also consider what's in another household pet's pantry— they have been known to put away a box of dry cat food or two.

A lot of hamsters like alfalfa, and you can get the natural form of alfalfa treat squares, which are also natural, but prepared. Consisting of 100% natural dehy-drated alfalfa, alfalfa treats provide necessary fiber roughage, and the hard surfaces are also helpful in maintaining your hamster's teeth.

One thing most all of these foods and snacks have in common is that

Setting up shop for hamsters. This new pet owner is giving the hamster's bedding a shot of disinfectant to discourage parasites and disease organisms. Photo by Susan C. Miller.

Many commercial hamster and small animal food mixes offer a wide variety of seeds, nuts and pellets for more complete nutrition. Photo by Michael Gilroy.

they are meatless. The viewpoint of many breeders and owners of hamsters is that hamsters don't need meat, and that you shouldn't give it to them. Other hamster owners claim that they have been able to feed their pets bits of cooked meat (never raw meat) such as chicken and turkey and other leftovers from the family dinner table. Again, some pets go an entire lifetime without sampling the family's own food fare, getting only the basics. Other pets in other houses almost have a place set for them every night— or morning (some hamsters get scrambled eggs from one hamster owner)—at the family's table.

SOFT VERSUS DRY FOODS

Here's an area where some disagreement might develop between hamster owners. Scrambled

eggs, chicken and other "soft" foods, some contend, are not the right things to serve a hamster. One reason is because these foods can't be hoarded— and hamsters like to hoard food. If they are hoarded, they will spoil and bacteria will build up inside the cage.

The counter argument is that you can serve hamsters these foods, if you give them small bits at a time. That way, they say, the hamster won't get a chance to hoard anything where it might spoil.

This argument carries over into the area of vegetable supplements too. Because most of the commercially prepared hamster food products contain certain amounts of vegetable ingredients, such as ground corn, soybean meal, alfalfa, ground oats and other vegetables, some hamster owners are quite content to serve only these store-bought food products.

Others will serve the actual vegetables themselves to the hamster. Recommended vegetables for the hamster include carrots, spinach, lettuce, potatoes and corn. Individual hamster tastes vary here too. Some hamster owners say that their pets like these and other things like apple slices, grapes and bananas; others say not. Why not give your hamster a sampling of different foods to find out what he likes?

It must also be mentioned here that these days a lot of the fruits and vegetables bought at the supermarket and local produce stand are grown with the use of pesticides. Be sure to wash thoroughly any fruits and vegetables that you are going to give to your hamster. And be sure to check the cage when these foods are served, so they do not remain there, where they can spoil.

The same thing would apply to anything grown in your own garden or a neighbor's garden. Wash this food too, because many of your neighbors may be using chemical companies to spray their lawns and yards with toxic pesticides, and these chemicals may drift into your garden.

Always serve food that is fresh. While dry food won't spoil as quickly as fruits, vegetable, dairy, and meat products, you should always check its age by looking at the food processor's milling date on the box. Pellets, seeds, seed mixes, and other dry foods that have been around too long can also go bad, and this "old" food can make your hamster sick. If dry foods are stored in damp cellars or other damp places, they

Even though hamsters enjoy nuts of various types, these foodstuffs should not make up the bulk of a hamster's diet. Photo by Michael Gilroy.

Hamsters must have water available at all times. The most convenient way of accomplishing this is to supply your hamster's house with a water bottle. Photo courtesy of Penn Plax.

can also lose their crispness. Always store these dry foods in a dry place.

WATER IS ESSENTIAL

It is vital that the hamster get a constant supply of fresh, clean drinking water. It should be placed in a clean water bottle and attached to the hamster's cage. Make sure the bottle doesn't leak or spill. Most water bottles are sturdy enough to withstand the hamster's gnawing. However, it would be a good practice to check on the water bottle

frequently to see if it is working properly. And as added insurance that your hamster gets all the water he needs, especially if you are going to be away for any length of time, you might want to toss an apple slice or bit of raw potato in his cage; both contain extra moisture.

SNACKS AND TREATS

Besides being another source of food, hamster treats and snacks provide a number of useful functions. These snacks and treats come in all shapes and sizes, and one thing they do is add some more variety to the animal's basic diet.

These commercially prepared treats are usually in dry form and don't create any problems

Nature's Little Greenhouse

For a healthy pet grow fresh organic greens

Fun for your whole family

associated with perishable snacks, such as those from the dinner or breakfast table.

Hamster snacks and treats also ensure that your pet gets all the nutrients he needs. It is possible that he is not getting them from his regular diet. For example, fiber roughage should be a part of your hamster's basic diet. If you are having trouble getting this for your pet, there are 100% natural dehydrated alfalfa treats which will provide it. There are also other combinations of dehydrated vegetables in the form of snacks or treats, some of which can be added to the hamster's regular food each day. There are even cheese-flavored hamster food supplements formulated to supply your pet with additional sources of protein.

Most pets like crunchy treats, and the hamster is no exception. Besides being tasty, they help to keep his teeth in good condition. Most crunchy treats and snacks also contain ingredients enriched with vitamins and minerals.

Whether they are in the form of squares or wafers, crispy sticks or cookies, hamster snacks and treats are meatless for the most part, containing various combinations of green vegetables, sunflower seeds, grain, natural honey, alfalfa, and other assortments of dehydrated vegetables.

This is not to say that you can't find your own additional snacks and treats around the house.

Hamsters have been known to consume a dog biscuit or two. They also like some cereals. But, again, snacks should be crunchy and not so quick to spoil as soft foods.

VITAMINS

Vitamins are also important to the well-being of hamsters. A vitamin deficiency can result in nervousness, inactivity, loss of hair, weight loss and other problems.

Adding one or two drops of hamster vitamins to the pet's daily diet will help to maintain resistance to illness and disease. Vitamins also help to bring out the soft, lustrous beauty of the animal's fur. And, of course, vitamins also help to ensure that your pet gets all the vital nutrients that he needs. Vitamin E is particularly important for the hamster.

Still other food items, such as the commercially made "lickstone," provide salt and trace elements of zinc, manganese, iron, copper, iodine, and cobalt. The lickstone is a round spool which can be hung from the wires of the hamster's cage. A mineral block is also a source of all

This rear-end view of a plump golden hamster clearly illustrates the animal's hoarding capability.

of the elements found in the lickstone. The stone or mineral block is also larger than the lickstone and should be placed somewhere on the floor of the cage. The blocks provide another outlet for the hamster to wear down its teeth safely. Such items are available at your local pet shop.

HOARDING

People like hamsters as pets for a number of reasons, one of which is the interesting way the animal stuffs his cheek pouches with food and then scurries away — looking like a balloon with feet—to hoard it.

The hamster doesn't overeat. (You can, however,

Above and left: Hamsters can be offered crickets and mealworms as a source of animal protein. **Below:** Rawhide Oodles™ are good for hamsters for a number of reasons. Made of the highest quality rawhide that's been melted and molded and cut into pieces, they make excellent gnaw snacks that help keep this rodent's teeth at their proper length. They taste good, and they are a good size for hoarding in a cheek!

put too much weight on him by feeding him too many things from the family dinner or breakfast table. Red meat morsels easily put weight on your hamster.) Whether you feed him once a day at a set time, or simply refill his food supply when it starts getting low, you will find that the hamster will eat when he wants to eat, and he will hide the rest away to nibble on when he's hungry again.

Hamsters have different hoarding styles. A female hamster expecting a litter is a particularly busy hoarder. You should make sure that the female, if she is expecting a litter, gets all the food and water she wants, because one of the problems associated with the hamster breeding cycle and weaning period involves a lack of nourishment. If a mother is not getting the right nutrition and the right amount of food for herself and her litter—or if she starts to think that she isn't —she could become even more nervous, to the point where she might devour her young. And, of course, if the hamster mother herself does not get the right nourishment and dies, then the hamster litter will not be able to survive either.

Your average nervous hamster or one who has been moved around a lot recently will stuff his pouches until he looks like some strange pet from another planet.

Most hamsters try to keep their hoard in one place in the cage, usually somewhere near where they sleep and as far away as possible from where they make their toilet. However, some hamster owners find that this is not always necessarily so—they find that their pet is using several areas in the cage for his toilet. Possibly, this might be because the cage itself has not been kept as clean as it should. Always make sure that the cage has been furnished with enough wood shavings, not only for sleeping and toilet areas but for food hoarding "kitchens" as well.

LIVE FOOD?

Then there is the question of live food. Hamsters in their native habitat eat insects, which provide a source of protein. But a pet hamster is *not* living in his native state and the question is: do you *have* to go out and get insects and give them to your pet in order for him to get *all* the natural nourishment he needs?

The good news for those who don't want to do this is that it is not necessary. Commercially prepared hamster chow supplies the animal with proper nutrition, and added nutrients can be made up in the form of snacks, fruits and vegetables, and vitamins.

But if you do want to supply your pet with live food and make him feel like he's back home in the desert, give him mealworms. Pet stores and specialty shops also carry crickets and grasshoppers. These, however, do cost a little more

Any greenfood that you serve to your hamster should be fresh and free of pesticides. Photo by Michael Gilroy.

money. If you decide to serve this kind of "natural" diet to your hamster, you would serve him two per day along with his normal food.

Don't get beetles and other insects from your backyard or from anywhere other than a specialty shop unless you're absolutely sure that the insects haven't eaten insecticides. And again, these days with so many of your neighbors using pesticides and other toxic substances on lawns, trees and shrubs, it's very difficult to know exactly what's on or in the ground or drifting into your yard. And moving from the ground to the flying creatures, don't ever give your hamster flies because they are carriers of disease.

CHEWING AND GNAWING

Gnawing sticks not only have a coating of tasty ingredients and seeds, but they also help keep the hamster's teeth trim and healthy: when the seeds are gone, the remaining wooden center is a good gnawing stick. Gnawing and chewing are vital activities for all members of the rodent family. Guinea pigs, mice, rabbits, gerbils, and hamsters all have teeth which grow during their entire life.

This constant growth must be worn away by gnawing before the teeth get too long. Overgrown teeth can lead to an inability to chew properly. In extreme cases, hamsters have died of starvation even when there was enough food available. Others have developed lesions and sores because of overgrown teeth.

The vital importance of keeping their teeth in perfect shape helps to explain why hamsters are always gnawing on things. A hamster will chew on his cage, the metal or glass end of a water bottle, food dishes and whatever else he can get his teeth into— in the cage or out of the cage. To keep his teeth in shape and to keep the damage he

can cause to a minimum, provide a good variety of gnawing aids in food and non-food form.

MEAT FOR THE HAMSTER?

Does giving hamsters meat, especially red meat, help to bring out the cannibalism that they sometimes resort to during the breeding cycle? There's no absolute answer to that question. The general census, however, is that most people *do not* recommend meat as part of a hamster's diet.

Considering the fact that the hamster is getting laboratory tested and scientifically prepared nourishment from his regular com- mercial chow, he doesn't really *need* meat.

Whatever food a hamster doesn't finish at mealtime will be hoarded away for subsequent snacking. Photo by Michael Gilroy.

HANDLING THE HAMSTER

Because he is a caged animal, many people might think the hamster should simply be left in his cage and, of course, fed and given water and clean bedding from time to time. This is *not* the case—one should handle the animal frequently. Two basic points should be made in this regard. One is that you should handle the pet

The hamster is one small animal to which the terms "cute and cuddly" can definitely be applied. Handled properly, a hamster will almost never bite. Photo by Vince Serbin.

hamster in order to build up a "relationship"; the more you handle the hamster, the more familiar he will become with you, the more he will trust and respond to you, and the better pet he will be. The second aspect is the correct way of handling your hamster. The hamster is quick, moves around a lot and is sometimes hard to "get a handle on," but there are correct ways to handle him. Incorrect handling will only frighten and possible injure your pet.

First of all, *never* handle, touch, breathe on or even go near baby hamsters until they have been weaned. This takes place about three or four weeks after they are born. If baby hamsters are touched before this time, there is a very good chance that the mother hamster will devour them.

Next, try to find time to play with the hamster during *his* normal waking hours. This would be in the evening and at night. If you do choose to spend time with your hamster during the day, be sure to wake him up gently—he'll probably be sleeping soundly!—and keep him out of any bright light. Let him awaken fully and then let him get used to you.

Don't put your hand *over* the hamster because you may frighten him. Hamsters are naturally friendly creatures and they will be friendly and curious

When holding your pet hamster, cradle it in your hands, rather than attempt to confine it by grasping the animal. Photo by Bonnie Buys.

An occupied hamster is a happy hamster. Toys, in fact, can be considered essential cage items as they contribute to your pet's well being. Photo by Michael Gilroy.

as long as they are not startled. More often than not, bites from a hamster are caused by careless handling of the animal, or sometimes by movements on your part that are too fast for him to follow. A startled hamster will bite at a hand suddenly hovering over him. When you are petting or handling the animal, always let him know that you are there before you even attempt to pick him up.

Always be gentle. Let him gradually get used to you, to the sound of your voice, to the human smell of your hand. You want to reach a point where the hamster will respond to you and come to you on his own.

To make a hamster this friendly, you've got to spend a lot of time with him and handle him regularly. A new pet requires careful handling to build up trust, and that trust will increase. Like all animals, hamsters will bite, but there is less chance of that happening if they are handled regularly when they are young.

Remember that your hamster is, by nature, a gentle, friendly pet and that you too must be gentle and friendly and patient. Patience is very important. If you try to hurry things, you will only frighten him and you both will have to start all over again.

You should always be gentle when waking and handling the hamster, and you should also always proceed slowly. Offer your hand slowly, giving him plenty of time to identify you as a friend rather than as an enemy. If your pet is unusually jumpy, it might be best to start by offering him the back of your hand rather than easily bitten fingers. Allow the hamster to get used to your human smell and the appearance of your hand. Be patient.

When picking up your hamster, try to cup your

hands under and then over him so that he feels secure. Try not to be nervous or afraid because hamsters can detect this fear with their keen sense of smell and become nervous themselves.

Don't let the hamster escape; this will make him more jittery and he could fall and injure himself. Hamsters don't have good vision and they easily misjudge distances and heights.

Always give your pet support from below. You may feel more comfortable holding him in hands clasped beneath him and thumbs forming a kind of roof over his head. Allow the hamster to walk into your handmade "cave" and

then gradually, but not *too* gradually, tighten them around him.

You can also cradle the hamster in the crook of your arm. That way he's not dangling. It is not recommended that you carry your pet around by the scruff of his neck, despite the fact that his skin is loose and stretches. If this needs to be done in case of an emergency, always support the animal from underneath. Hamsters are fragile, and the spine should be protected from any unnecessary twisting or bending.

Use common sense when you are handling or playing with the hamster. Never leave it alone and unsupervised while it is out of the cage. Be sure an

"Here's looking at you!" A wild-colored golden hamster takes in the view from his owner's hand. Photo by Burkhard Kahl.

Apple, as well as any other kind of fruit, should be fed only in limited quantity. Photo by Michael Gilroy.

adult is present if a young, inexperienced child is handling the hamster. Make sure that there is nothing around that the animal can fall on and injure himself. Remember, a hamster has very poor vision, and he relies more on his sense of smell than his eyesight to get around.

TAMING

Taming is a more sophisticated aspect of pet handling. While the objective of correctly handling the hamster is for you to help the animal get used to you—and *not* bite— the objective of taming is to make the animal friendly. Handling him will eventually lead to a point where he will trust you.

As is often the case in any part of the animal world, one of the keys to the taming of the

hamster is in the ritual of "breaking bread" with the animal. In other words, you can break the ice and build up friendship with him a lot more easily if you have a hamster snack or treat to offer.

There are at least two schools of thought when it comes to the pet owner's relationship to a pet. Some pet owners want to "command" their pets. Their goal, it often seems, is to give orders like a marine drill sergeant and make the animal *obey* those orders, sometimes, it seems, just for the sake of doing so. Taming, in our sense of the word, implies creating a working relationship between the pet owner and the pet to make everything easier, whether it's feeding, health care, maintenance of the cage or just everyday contact. You want to develop a rapport with your pet so that you can work as a team to get things done. And one of the things to accomplish is a spirit of cooperation. You can, actually, reach a point where you'll have the hamster voluntarily eating out of your hand.

HAMSTER HEALTH CARE

With the right kind of care, hamsters should not get sick much during their short life spans because they are naturally hardy and naturally resistant to disease and illness. However, they are also victimized by the same types of ailments that plague humans, and for some of the same reasons. They don't usually get sick, but if they do, it will probably be with the common cold and other upper respiratory maladies. The best thing you can do, as you can for yourself, is to practice a little bit of preventive medicine. To prevent the hamster from catching cold, make sure that the cage is situated away from all drafts. In the winter, make sure that all

A fine, mature specimen of the golden hamster, showing the rich coloration that has made it so popular as a housepet. Photo by Michael Gilroy.

Russian hamster. A hamster relies greatly on his sense of smell when investigating objects that are foreign to him. Photo by Michael Gilroy.

the storm windows are in place and that the hamster's room temperature stays in the 65 to 72°F (18-22°C) range. In extremely cold spells you might want to add an extra layer of insulation under the animal's cage, and you might even want to put a blanket over the top of the cage—making sure, however, that the hamster won't be able to chew on it, and making sure that the blanket doesn't stop the proper air circulation.

In the summertime, make certain that the pet isn't too close to air conditioning vents or fans.

ROOM TEMPERATURE

Moderation is the word when you're talking about the right room temperature for hamsters. Ideally, the golden hamster should be put in a cage, in a room where the temperature is between 65 and 72°F (18-22°C). Dwarf hamsters like it a little cooler.

Temperatures can drop below the 65°F (18°C) mark if the

hamster's cage is furnished with an extra supply of pine or cedar shavings. This allows the animal to burrow or dig a little deeper and get that extra warmth.

Of course, you don't want the temperature to drop *too* low—50°F (10°C) would be way too low—because the hamster might not be able to burrow deep enough to get that extra warmth and he may go into a state of hibernation. He will sleep, the body will get rigid and his own body temperature will fall below normal. To bring him out of hibernation, put him in your hands and warm him up. Turn up the heat—not too warm, not above 72°F (22°C) and let in some sunshine. Normally, hamsters don't like sunlight, but in this case a little bit won't hurt.

The only time you might keep the temperature up a little higher is during the breeding and weaning cycles.

Always keep in mind that the hamster in your home is in a very different environment than his natural, native surroundings. In the desert, where the Syrian, or golden, hamster is originally from, temperatures range from 100°F (38°C) and up during the day to the low

30s (0°C) at night. However, in that environment, the hamster knows how and where to go to keep warm or cool. In man-made situations you have to help him out.

While the hamster, for the sake of his health, should be warm enough and should not be placed near any drafts where he could catch cold, his cage and surroundings should

also be kept clean and dry. Remove food so that it doesn't get moldy. Check the hamster's cheek pouches to make sure that foods don't get stuck in them—foods which can spoil and cause bacteria to

One of the health problems rodents face is that their teeth, which are constantly growing, can get too long, causing pain and irritation. Given something hard and chewy, like a Chick-N-Cheez Oodle, your hamster can get a workout for his teeth while enjoying a tasty, healthy snack. Oodles are 100% digestible.

build up. Water bottles should also be kept scrupulously clean and water should always be fresh and not too cold.

WET TAIL

Wet tail is one of the most destructive diseases that a hamster can get. There are several theories on the causes of wet tail,

The fact that all of the water tubes in this overcrowded holding cage are always in use points out the hamster's constant need for ample water! Photo by Bonnie Buys.

none absolutely conclusive, but one contributing factor in the disease and in the spread of the disease may be a build-up of dampness and humidity in the hamster's environment.

Some say that wet tail can occur after shipping or when hamsters have been crowded together too long in an inadequate cage. Overheating may also contribute to the problem because heat allows the infectious germs to multiply rapidly at a time when the animals are most

susceptible to the germs.

Wet tail is also very contagious and can be spread by contaminated water from one hamster to the next. It can also be spread by simple contact. The symptoms are much the same as diarrhea, only much more severe. Hamsters hit with this disease must be treated immediately if they are going to have any chance of making it through. The main killer in the disease is dehydration due to diarrhea. To combat this, fluids must be readily available and within easy reach of the afflicted one, who, if struck by wet tail, will become emaciated and weak as the backside area gets wet and discolored.

Do all that you can do to prevent this disease from striking. Besides keeping the cage clean and dry, make sure the bedding—wood shavings—in the cage is also dry from the surface to the bottom of the cage. This, however, poses still another problem in the entire wet tail dilemma. You are supposed to keep the hamster's cage as clean and dry as possible, but you have to do it in such a way that you won't upset the inhabitant. If you move things around *too* much or *too* often, you could cause the hamster to experience a certain amount of stress.

One theory views stress as a contributing factor in a hamster's succumbing to wet tail. This stress can be caused by a number of things, including excessive cleaning and disruption of the animal's cage or it can result from the hamster's inability to adjust to a new home. Any animal would be nervous at first in a new home, and an unlucky hamster might find himself in a home where children are always grabbing him, picking him up and dropping him, making loud noises and frightening him, turning on lights that are too bright, bringing in other animals, opening windows that allow too much cold air to enter, etc.

If wet tail does become a problem for your hamster, you should thoroughly clean and disinfect his entire cage, including the frame, the feeding dishes and bottles, toys, exercise wheel and anything else of his or yours in the surrounding area in order to slow the spread of the disease

immediately. You should even consider throwing away some of these items and getting new dishes, water bottles and gnawing sticks. Of course, you must destroy old litter, bedding and food, and put new shavings, fresh food and water in the cage after it has been thoroughly disinfected.

If hamsters are exposed to food which has spoiled, minor intestinal problems (at least compared to wet tail they are minor) may result. You can usually tell by the hamster's stool how healthy he is. Normal, solid droppings indicate that all is well. If his stomach is upset or if he is afflicted with other, more serious maladies, the droppings

A golden hamster with a thirst takes his turn at the water tube. Photo by Bonnie Buys.

will likely be loose and watery. This could indicate anything from minor—too much dairy consumption, too many fruits and vegetables or ingestion of spoiled foods—to the more serious intestinal disorders.

Conversely, the animals may also suffer from constipation. Constipation in young or adult hamsters can result from too many dry pellets and not enough water. If you give your hamster dry pellets, you must provide plenty of fresh drinking water. If you have more than one hamster, make sure that one animal does not take all the water. In case of constipation, give young hamsters some greens and give adult hamsters carrots, leafy vegetables and fruit.

The same problems can develop when water is offered to the hamster in an open dish instead of in a standard water bottle. He might accidentally contaminate his drinking water with feces or rotting food. When contaminated water is imbibed, many of the symptoms are similar to the intestinal problems related to food spoilage. While some specially-made hamster diarrhea aids, as well as human diarrhea aids, can help cure these ills, the best prevention is the use of closed water bottles.

Diarrhea is also a common problem developed during shipping, so it would be very wise for you to completely look over your animal in the pet store and to make sure he is healthy before you bring him home. Always check for signs of diarrhea and staining; if these are present, it is not a good idea to move the animal until the problem has been corrected.

COLDS

From upset stomachs we go to upper respiratory problems. The symptoms of a cold are inactivity and ruffled fur; the hamster's nose might look a little swollen, too, because he may be constantly wiping the nasal discharge on his fur. He may also sniffle and sneeze, lose a little weight and lose a little luster on his coat. Loss of weight and ruffled coat are always signs that something is wrong.

Ruffled coat, loss of appetite, rapid breathing, nasal discharge, coughing and sneezing could also be signs of more severe respiratory problems and the onset of pneumonia.

Respiratory problems can develop in malnourished groups of damp

There was an old hamster who lived in a shoe. . . Hamsters are intrigued by toys that offer snug and secluded hiding places. Photo by Michael Gilroy.

and/or overcrowded animals. Poor air circulation could be another contributing factor. If you are planning to house your hamster in a tank (as opposed to a commercially designed hamster cage or bird-cage, both of which are much more "open"), make sure that there is enough ventilation. One argument against the use of a tank for a hamster home is the fact that some tanks may not allow the proper air flow, which builds up not only heat but humidity as well and may result in a certain amount of dampness in the hamster's living quarters. And as humidity builds up in the now stuffy hamster home, the animal's own body may start to generate too much heat, partly out of stress because of this change in the environment. All of this builds up in the tank as well. And, on top of all this, the resulting change for the worse in the hamster's home might cause even further stress, making him that much more susceptible to the germs building up all around him.

Therefore, preventing the development of these and other conditions, and their consequences, is always the first thing to try to accomplish in respect of hamster health care. If, however, the animal does come down with something and treatment is necessary, treat colds and sniffles with plenty of fresh food, clean water, a clean, dry cage and warm, soft bedding.

Sometimes there may be false alarms. For example, after the hamster has packed away one two many pellets in his cheek pouches, his eyes may start to tear, and it may look like he's starting to get a cold. This could simply be owing to the fact that some food has stuck in one of the animal's cheek pouches. To get excess food out of the cheek pouches, try using a medicine dropper filled with warm water to flush out the debris in the pouches.

FLEAS AND MITES

Skin parasites are not common on pet hamsters, but if they do infest yours there's a good chance that he got them from another household pet, such as a cat or dog; both are more susceptible to the attack of fleas, lice, ticks, and mites.

If you have other animals in the house, the best thing to do for the well-being of all your pets, and for you, is to control parasites by using medications in spray or powder form. If you have a dog or a cat with a bad case of fleas, you should take him to a veterinarian or animal grooming specialist and have the pests removed with a special dip before they go from your pets to the furniture and the rest of the house and reach the hamster's cage.

CUTS AND WOUNDS

Hamsters are very playful, especially when they are young, but they are also capable of violent and vicious fighting during the courting and mating cycle in particular. Female hamsters at this time are quite capable of killing male hamsters. Serious fighting

Most of the minor squabbles among hamsters involve food or a lack of adequate "personal space." Photo by Michael Gilroy.

should always be detected by you and stopped as quickly as possible. When you hear the hamster's teeth chattering or when you hear the hamster shrieking, you know that he is involved in a serious altercation or that one is about to

two cages, one for the male and one for the female. You would never, during the mating cycle, put the male hamster into the female hamster's cage, nor would you leave him there after the mating is over. (The male hamster might kill the baby hamsters.) The best roommates are young male hamsters

A ball of rope makes a satisfactory hideaway for this young hamster. Photo by Michael Gilroy.

break out very soon. Baby hamsters playing in the nest make tiny squeaking sounds, which are usually no cause for alarm.

The best way to prevent fighting—and serious bites and cuts—is to match the animals up correctly as roommates in the first place. If you are going to breed hamsters, you need

from the same litter. The female hamster, whether she is having a litter or not, should live alone in her own cage. And if you are going to have two male hamsters share the same cage, you will cut down on the chances of fighting by giving them a cage that is big enough for them to keep out of each other's way. Of course, if each hamster has his or her own cage, there will rarely be cuts, wounds, or bites to worry about—unless the hamster gnaws on something in the cage and gets splinters.

The hamster can reach his cuts and wounds with his tongue, and his constant licking of the wound will normally keep it from getting infected. If the cut or wound doesn't seem

are likely to attack him.

While minor scrapes and illnesses can result from contact with other healthy animals in your home, contact with contaminated animals can be fatal to your hamster. You must do your part to make sure that wild rats or mice cannot get near your hamster's cage because they are carriers of a host of other parasitical diseases.

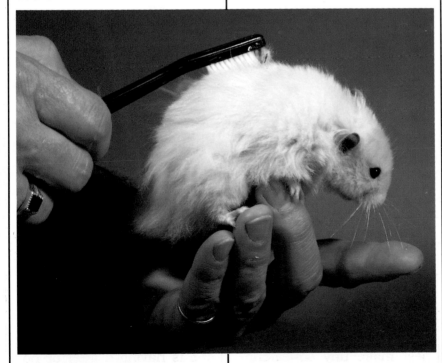

An ordinary toothbrush makes a perfectly acceptable hamster grooming tool. Photo by Ron and Val Moat.

to be getting any better, treat it with an antiseptic applied with a cotton swab. More serious cuts and wounds should be looked at by the veterinarian. A wounded animal should never be kept in a cage with other animals, as they

Household pests like roaches, bedbugs, and mites can sometimes get into hamster cages, especially in urban areas or regions where there is a lot of heat and humidity. Get rid of them. Use insecticides, if necessary,

Hamsters are notoriously fond of squeezing into various nooks and crannies. Photo by Michael Gilroy.

but when doing so remove the hamster from his cage and put him in a temporary home, a spare tank with a wire-screen top or an old bird cage. You might want to keep a small animal pen around the house for these and other emergencies. Put the hamster in his temporary home and take him to

another room, away from the noxious chemicals you are using. Disinfect the cage thoroughly, get rid of all old litter, food, water, and chewing sticks and replace them with new ones. Thoroughly clean the hamster's toys—the exercise wheel, the tubes and slides in the cage. If your hamster playground is an intricately designed system, you will have to take it apart and give every nook and cranny a thorough cleaning.

If the problem is serious, you might even take the trouble to put the cage out in the fresh air to aerate it completely. While you are doing this, don't forget to clean the room itself. Open all the windows to get rid of the chemical toxins in the air after the pest problem has been eliminated. Return the cage to the room and the hamster to his cage only when you are sure that everything is perfectly insect-free, clean and dry again.

While bacteria, viruses, and disease can be transmitted to hamsters from other animals, you too, as owner of several pets, could also be a transmitter of bacteria and disease to your hamster. Always wash your hands *before* as well as *after* you handle your pet.

ACTIVITY

One sign that an animal is ill is a lack of activity or a drop in activity on his part. Hamsters are subject to several different forms of paralysis. While the state of hibernation or cold paralysis may result from a drop in temperature, another form of hamster paralysis may be caused by a lack of exercise. Keep your hamster in a cage that has enough room for him and for any other hamster with which he is sharing the cage and make sure that the cage is equipped with an exercise wheel or some other piece of exercise equipment that will encourage him to stay active.

Still another form of paralysis may result from a vitamin deficiency. Vitamin E, a much-needed vitamin, is found in peanuts, and vitamin D is found in wheat germ and wheat germ oil.

The more familiar you are with your hamster's behavior the better you will be able to tell when he is not feeling well. Photo by Michael Gilroy.

THE HAMSTER'S TEETH

The hamster's teeth can also create unusual problems. While they are always growing throughout the animal's life, his teeth can decay. To help prevent dental problems, give the hamster one or several gnawing aids to keep the teeth in proper condition.

The constant growth of the hamster's teeth must be worn away by gnawing before the teeth get too long. If the teeth get too long they could lead to an inability on the animal's part to chew properly. In extreme cases, hamsters have died of starvation even when they had enough food available. In less extreme cases, lesions and sores can result from overgrown teeth.

The need to keep their teeth in perfect shape helps to explain the constant preoccupation most hamsters have with gnawing during their entire life.

This attractive hamster gym is, unfortunately, made entirely of wood and thus won't last very long in the face of determined chewing by this active pair! Photo by Michael Gilroy.

A hamster will chew on anything—cage wires, the water bottle, food dishes and whatever else he can sink his teeth into. To minimize the damage the animal can cause to himself and to your home and his, provide him with a variety of gnawing aids.

Also, check to see that the hamster doesn't break any teeth during a fall or during one of his acrobatic stunts. If the hamster does have a very loose tooth, it can be removed. But this is really a job for your vet.

GROOMING

Pet owners like the fact that the hamster is a clean animal. He cleans himself all day, licking his paws to wash his face. He uses his paws and tongue to clean his belly, back and legs. The bath that the hamster gives himself, from head to toe, also serves to keep his coat of fur clean and shiny.

While the animal may even take several of these "baths" a day, you should make sure that the hamster isn't cleaning himself with nervous movements, as this could indicate that something is bothering him, the presence of another animal, for example.

You might see the hamster preening the fur around the tiny gland he has on each hip. These glands secrete small quantities of a fluid something like musk. It does not mean that anything is wrong if he is spending a lot of time preening the fur around this gland.

OLD AGE

Hamsters that are well cared for, handled properly and fed nutritionally balanced meals, whose cages are kept clean and dry, may live up to or a bit longer than 1,000 days. Towards the end of his life,

Hamsters are fastidious groomers and will lick and clean their fur until it shines, as in this beautiful satin hamster. Photo by Michael Gilroy.

the hamster may start eating less and start sleeping more. If he seems to be comfortable and is not suffering from any pain, he should be allowed to live out his natural life in his cage. Treat him gently and feed him whatever he will eat. If, on the other hand, your hamster has developed a disease which makes him uncomfortable and causes him to experience pain, the humane thing to do is bring him to the veterinarian and have him painlessly euthanized.

A HAMSTER MISCELLANY

Just as you have to take care of the hamster and make sure that he gets the right food and enough drinking water, you will also have to be both maintenance person and housekeeper for his cage. While the hamster is naturally a clean animal, a cage is a man-made structure and needs human hands to attend to it. Two words—clean and dry—should always be on your mind when it concerns the hamster's environment.

The cage should be cleaned and the shavings changed about once a week. Use a mild natural soap for cage cleaning. All parts of the cage should be washed thoroughly. After cleaning the cage with soap, be sure to rinse all the soap residue away with clear clean water. When you are cleaning the cage, look for any leftover food that might be rotting in the cage. Clean that out immediately. Do not, however, disturb your hamster's hoard of dry pellets. If you upset his hoard, it is very likely you will also upset your hamster.

A cute pose but not a hamster's preferred habit, given a choice! Photo by Michael Gilroy.

When you're cleaning the cage, make sure the feeding dish is scrubbed. Food build-up can cause bacteria, which, in turn, could upset your hamster's stomach.

The hamster's droppings, normally dry and hard, are usually left in one area. Some hamster owners say that they find the animal's droppings all over the cage. *Generally,* the hamster will use one corner of his cage for his toilet and another for sleeping and hoarding. The toilet area should be cleaned out every day and new litter should be added. It is especially important to keep wetness from building up from the urine. When you clean and remove old shavings, always be sure to put enough new shavings back into the cage.

While the toilet area should be cleaned daily (wet litter removed), the hamster's sleeping area should be cleaned and changed once or twice a week. Replace all the litter in the urinal area every two or three days. When you're making the hamster's bed and cleaning his cage, put him somewhere else, possibly in another small pan filled with shavings, or let him play on his exercise wheel.

Once a month, you should give the entire cage, and everything in it, a thorough cleaning.

Take everything out and air it out, possible on your back porch.

Recently weaned hamsters develop natural toilet habits. The only thing that a "housekeeper" should be aware of is that the urine might dry a bit more quickly and it might not have a noticeable odor...at first. Baby hamsters should get a little more bedding and litter.

SHOULD THE HAMSTER BE LET OUT OF HIS CAGE?

This is another question individual hamster owners, with different styles of handling pets, will have to answer for themselves. Some people are quite content to leave their pets in their cage at all times, never letting them out. Other hamster owners let their pets out to play with them or even to set on their laps and watch TV.

If you are thinking of giving the hamster a little more room to run around in every now and then, please consider these factors: other animals in the house; small children, infants, toddlers in the house; open windows; and open doors.

Under the right conditions and with good supervision, the hamster can be let out of his cage. Wait until he is used to your house. Don't let him out of his cage the day you bring him home . . . or the next day. Wait until he gets the feel of the place and becomes familiar with you. Always start animals

A simple, but adequate, sleeping box, filled with cedar shavings. Photo by Michael Gilroy.

Hamsters and avian pets don't really mix, though these two conures certainly seem intrigued by the antics of the little rodents! Photo by Michael Gilroy.

out with small areas, gradually expanding their territory.

It therefore follows that you should limit the hamster to the exploration of one room. Close all windows. Make sure the door is closed. Make sure he won't be able to get under the door. Seal off closets and air vents as well. And, of course, be there at all times.

The best time to let your hamster run around is usually in the evening. Most of all, it should be at a time when things have quieted down around your house. You don't want people coming in and out, opening and shutting windows, slamming doors, making a lot of noise. It should be at a quiet time of the day when everything is relaxed.

Hamsters can damage things found around the house. They might chew electrical wires and extensions, wires that hook up to stereos and speakers. Never give a hamster a chance to get near electric cords and other wiring, as this can create a possibly dangerous situation for everyone. Hamsters can

also get into upholstered furniture and disappear under a sofa or a chair. They might chew on wallpaper, especially loose wallpaper. They also chew books, clothing, and newspaper.

You don't want your animal to fall into anything that's filled with water, like a vase or a pail. A hamster can climb and get into the unlikeliest of places. He can also fall from them, and that can be harmful to his health.

HAMSTERS AND OTHER PETS?

Caution is the word when it comes to mixing hamsters and other pets. It can be done under *very* close and strict supervision. Yes, hamsters *can* do so and have made friends with the cat of the house to the point where he even crawls on the cat's back. But you have to remember that cats also eat hamsters, and there's a good chance they will if you're not around to supervise.

Dogs will go after hamsters too. A very well-trained dog will probably refrain from going after the hamster if you're there. But it's better not to put them together.

Don't forget, too, that while you are protecting the hamster, You are creating a certain amount of stress on the part of the other pets in the house by your rigid supervision and control of what normally would be their natural behavior.

Besides keeping animals apart, make sure that the

hamster's cage is securely protected and positioned in the room so that these animals can not claw through the bars or knock the entire cage over.

If you have other small mammals—other hamsters, mice, gerbils, rabbits—always remember to wash your hands with soap before going from one animal to another for feeding or playing. The odor of other rodents may

Perfect camouflage is not the word here! But care *is* the word when allowing any pet hamster to explore on its own. They have a talent for disappearing acts! Photo by Ron and Val Moat.

A hamster and a gerbil get to know each other. Always supervise your hamster when he is in the company of other household pets. Photo by Michael Gilroy.

excite hamsters to the point where they'll snap or even suddenly attack their cage-mate, if they have one.

IF THE HAMSTER ESCAPES

Do all that you can do to prevent the hamster from escaping in the first place. See that his cage is secure, that all the bars in it are not too wide apart. The hamster is always looking for ways to get in and out of things.

But if your hamster *does* escape, what will you do? Whatever you do, don't conduct an unorganized, noisy search for the animal. This might frighten him and make him even more difficult to find.

The first thing you should do is to look everywhere you think he could possibly be— anywhere he could hide— under a sofa, *in* the upholstery of a sofa, or a chair. This is why it is a

much better idea to keep the hamster, if you do let him out of the cage from time to time, confined to one room in your home. If that room is securely sealed, it will make your search for the missing hamster that much easier—he has to be somewhere in that room.

Incidentally, you should make sure that this room doesn't have any loose boards or holes in the walls that the hamster can fit through.

Food is often very useful in helping an animal find his way back home. Try using a piece of carrot or some sunflower seeds or some of the hamster's favorite snacks to lure him back. Try opening the cage and filling it with an extra supply of his favorite food. Leave the room and check from time to time to see if he has returned on his own.

Be very careful not to allow your hamster to escape to the outdoors. There will be plenty of cats in the neighborhood just looking for something like this to take place.

BREEDING

Hamsters reproduce faster than any other mammal. Their gestation period is an average of 16 days. The female

hamster is ready to mate every four days, and when she gives birth the litter ranges from two to 15, with seven baby hamsters the average litter. She is ready to mate again when the baby hamsters are about 30 days old. However, it is recommended that she be given more time. The female hamster can normally produce more than four litters, but four good litters is satisfactory.

The novice should not casually entertain the idea of breeding hamsters. While large-scale hamster breeding operations involve thousands of hamsters that are cared for by professionals, you too will have to take a very

professional attitude toward the task of breeding just one pair of hamsters.

The first thing you will have to do is to go out and get another cage. You will need one cage for the male hamster and another cage for the female hamster and the litter. The male hamster should be separated from the female and the baby hamsters because he might kill the baby hamsters. The female hamster will harm, and possibly kill, the male hamster as well.

Of course, you will have to clean each cage and supply each with enough wood shavings, pellets and water, and exercise equipment. In addition to

This gaggle of golden hamsters includes two adults and young of various ages.

this, you will have to supply nesting materials during the breeding cycle.

While the female hamster is capable of breeding at an earlier age, it is best that she be between ten and 12 weeks old before you mate her with the male hamster,

who should be a little older and a little more experienced. Dwarf hamsters should be three to four months old for breeding purposes. Breed only healthy animals. Young, malnourished females should not be used for breeding, and if a female's first litter is small you should not mate her again.

The mating activity should take place in the male hamster's cage. Never—but never—put the male hamster into the female hamster's cage! She will probably attack at once. Put the female in the male's cage. Normally, mating will take place at night or in the evening. After the mating is over, return the female to her own cage. Don't leave them together overnight. The female will not produce a bigger litter, and there's a good chance that she might hurt the male.

Hamsters might not hit it off the first time. This is normal. The female might start a fight with the male. Again, this is normal, even for a receptive female. If an

A hamster mating in progress. **Above:** The male follows the female with obvious interest. **Right:** He investigates the female's genital area.

altercation breaks out, get a pair of thickly padded gloves, put them on and return the female hamster to her own cage. In a day or so, bring her back and let them try it again. This method is particularly helpful to the male hamster, protecting him from the female and enabling him to be more productive throughout his breeding career. In fact, some commercial breeders avoid thesc one-on-one situations completely and use two males per female.

And while all of this is going on, don't plan any vacations. It is not advisable for you to call on a friend to take care of a hamster who is pregnant.

PREGNANCY

If the mating is successful, the golden hamster will deliver her litter in about 16 days; the Chinese and dwarf female hamsters take a few more days to deliver their young.

Once you determine that the female is pregnant, you should start getting ready to help her take care of the litter—not directly (she will do that), but by keeping her supplied with whatever she needs to give birth and raise the baby hamsters.

In the first place, how do you know if the female is pregnant? One sign may be a change in her normal routine. If you watch her closely, you might notice that she seems to be a lot busier than she normally is. She will be hoarding food, for herself and for the

The male mounts the female and coitus takes place rapidly. Photos by Ron and Val Moat.

A hamster mother attends to her brood; the babies are about 10 days old, as evidenced by their size and thin coat of fur. Photo by Michael Gilroy.

litter that she is expecting. Give her all the food she needs for hoarding, and also provide her with enough water. That water supply will be very important to the baby hamsters too. They must be able to reach the water bottle. In addition to food and water, the pregnant hamster should get a good supply of bedding—and, perhaps, equally important, she should have enough privacy.

Don't frighten or even startle her. Nervous, frightened females can react by devouring their young, something which they also might do if they are not getting the right amount of nourishment during their pregnancy.

Basically, the idea is for you to try to provide everything—or as much as can be provided—for the female hamster during her pregnancy and during weaning while, at the same time, staying out of her way.

Give a pregnant hamster all the nesting materials (whether they are of the commercial variety or pieces or burlap, which she will shred) that she needs to make a nest for her family.

A few days before the female is about to deliver would be about the right time for you to change the hamster shavings in the cage and to make the cage as clean and dry as possible. After this, you should leave the female alone as much as possible until about nine days after she has delivered her litter.

BABY HAMSTERS

The first thing that you should know, and keep in mind at all accidentally touch even one of the baby hamsters in the litter, even during an emergency, the mother may very well respond by destroying not just that one baby but her entire litter as well—a most unfortunate series of events which have been experienced by more than one pet hamster owner.

times, about baby hamsters is that you should leave them alone. The first nine or ten days in a baby hamster's life, and in the life of the mother, are critical in terms of his development *and* survival. If you

Left: This tiny youngster barely fills a bottle cap! **Below:** This snug nestful of babies illustrates the basic rodent method of concealing young from predators, though in nature grasses would be used rather than wood chips. Photos by Michael Gilroy.

Stages in a baby hamster's development: from top, newborn, five days, ten days, and two weeks. As in most other rodents, the development of the young is rapid; they are fully weaned in about 21 days. Photos by Michael Gilroy.

own home about the importance of leaving the hamster family alone at this time. You must ensure that little children, who will be curious about all of this, don't get near the cage and disturb the nest in any way. If you

Leave the hamster family alone as much as you possibly can. Keep the cage out of bright light and away from drafts, and put it in a cozy corner of a room that is a little warmer than usual. Don't make any noise near the cage. Do not attempt to clean the cage until ten days after the litter has been delivered. And at this time, just take out soiled shavings. Dead animals must always be removed immediately.

It is especially important at this time to ensure that the mother hamster has been well nourished and remains well nourished and calm, not frightened in any way. Also be sure to instruct everyone in your

have other household pets, such as a curious cat or two, you *must* be absolutely sure that these animals are kept away from the hamster's cage.

Newborn baby hamsters are born naked and blind. They are about one inch (2.6 cm) in length and they weigh between one-eighth and one-tenth of an ounce. (3.5-2.8 g). Dwarf hamsters may weigh about half as much. The babies start out as pink in color, and in about eight days they start growing hair. Their teeth are already formed at birth.

Although blind, baby hamsters move around quickly, guided mostly by their sense of smell and touch. Like cats, they have facial "whiskers" which act as sensors, enabling them to judge whether or not they can make it through a narrow space. When a baby hamster strays too far from the nest, the mother hamster takes hold of him or her in her mouth. The baby hamster stays still when he or she is being carried by the mother.

Baby hamsters squeak and squeal in the nest, making faint cries in minor skirmishes with other

Above: A cream hamster mom grooms one of her kids. **Below:** A weaned hamster kit at about one month. Photos by Michael Gilroy.

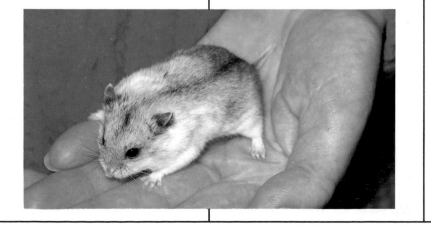

members of the litter over food and places at their mother's side. The mother hamster can hear these faint cries and she responds to them, especially if a young one seems to be calling for help or finding his way out of the nest.

The baby hamsters start to wander from the nest about ten days after they are born. The eyes are fully open at 12 days. Weaning is complete about 21 days after birth, and in a few more days the active and lively youngsters should be taken away from the mother.

This means another cage—*at least* another cage. So, at this point you will have the male hamster in one cage and the female or mother living alone in her cage. And then you will need a cage or cages for the young hamsters; hamster babies should be grouped according to sex at this point to prevent them from breeding when they are too young. The females in the litter should be placed in one cage, and the males of the litter should be placed in another. You can determine sex this way: the female will have two rows of seven mammae spots. The female's body is also rounder in the backside than the male's body, which has an extended rear with a bulge under the tail, where the testes are located. The

A dwarf hamster enjoying his meal. The heavy ceramic food dish shown here is the best overall for the hamster cage—easy-to-clean, sturdy and untippable. Photo by Michael Gilroy.

female hamster's vagina is close to the anus, while the male hamster's penis is much farther away from the anal opening.

Young hamsters should also be taken away from the mother at this time because she may, with or without becoming pregnant again, turn on her litter. If she is pregnant, this may happen because the female knows instinctively that she must now devote her full attention to the new litter she is expecting.

About the litter she has just delivered: after you have separated the males and the females and put them in separate cages, start looking for permanent homes for them. If you are going to keep two or three males of the same

litter in one cage, it is not a good idea to move one out then after a time to bring him back into the cage. By this time, the common bond, based on a common odor, will have disappeared. Certainly, by the time the fully-grown male hamster has reached his mature size—five to six inches (13-14 cm) in length and about five ounces (140 g) in weight—he should have his permanent home. Golden hamsters are fully grown at the age of three months, and dwarf hamsters at about two months. But they should have their permanent home long before this. A hamster should have a permanent home between five and eight weeks of age.

DIFFERENT TYPES OF HAMSTERS

When Henry Ford was selling some of his first automobiles, he told his customers that they could have any color that they wanted—as long as it was black. This is certainly not the "choice" someone looking for a hamster has to make.

Hamsters come in different sizes, with different "hairstyles" and in so many different colors and color patterns that "you can't even begin to describe nowadays," in the words of one

Your hamster's antics will delight you for hours on end. Photo by M. Gilroy.

commercial breeder of hamsters.

And yet it all started with one kind of a hamster—the Syrian, or golden, hamster, with his gold-colored fur and big black eyes. While this fellow is still around in great numbers, a number of different color varieties of hamster have been bred from this original hamster.

Hamsters today are bred in several basic

colors—from the all-white albino, with his pink eyes, to the black hamster, known for the light areas around his eyes, nose and feet.

But let's start with the

one has brown or ruby eyes.

Teddy Bear hamsters, also known as long-

Syrian hamster. His short hair is described as "agouti," which means natural wild colors of black and brown with various shades.

The base of the Syrian hamster's hair is dark blue-black; the middle layer of hair is brownish or golden; and the pointed tips of most of this hamster's hairs are black. In addition to these three distinct colors, the animal sports light gray belly fur with a few white patches.

The pied or harlequin or panda hamster has brown or beige spots on his coat. This dark-eyed hamster may need special care and patience because it is often a high-strung animal.

The opposite is true of the very popular, attractive, and lively and healthy cream-colored or fawn-colored hamster. This

haired or angora hamsters, look a little bit like tiny rock musicians with their long hair growing wildly. Though usually healthy, they are sometimes a bit frail in comparison with many of their hardier short-haired cousins.

Russian hamsters do not have pure white fur like the albino. The Russian hamster has dark stripes and marks on the tail and the ears.

The Chinese striped

A fine example of the banded hamster, an increasingly popular variety among pet owners. Photo by Michael Gilroy.

The long-haired hamster varieties are generally not a wise choice for the novice pet owner, as they require more attention to coat care and cage cleanliness. Photo by Michael Gilroy.

hamster is half the size of the Syrian hamster at maturity. When they are young, they have gray fur, and as they get older their coat turns brown.

The striped hairy-footed hamster has a gray-brown face in the summer; the ears are dark brown. This hamster has a dark brown stripe that runs down its back. The underfur is white, and the hamster's back feet are covered with fur.

Are some hamsters more gentle than others? Sometimes that depends on the kind of owner the hamster has, or the kind of care he gets. (It should also be noted that some hamsters are more high strung than others.)

In general, the color of the hamster should not be any true indication of any basic difference in the Syrian hamster family as a pet.

HAMSTER SHOWS

Almost every area of human endeavor—whether it's producing Broadway musicals or growing turnips—is highlighted by prize or award

A rust hamster.

Contented hamster and admirer. Photo by Dr. Herbert R. Axelrod.

cere-monies. One way hamster owners can compare their prize pets is through the national 4-H Club organization's Small Animal Club. The 4-H Clubs are organized on a county-by-county basis. Hamster shows are held in different places and at different times by the organization.

If you are thinking of entering your hamster in a show, bear in mind that the little guy will be judged and graded in several categories. Naturally, the hamster or hamsters you are entering in show competition should be a thing of beauty, with no patches or wounds. And, of course, points will be awarded for interesting colors.

Hamsters that have stolen many a show for their beauty include the long-haired white, the long-haired cinnamon, and the cream colored. Satin white and satin cream hamsters have also dazzled many a judge at a hamster show. Other show colors include the golden hamster, the beige, honey and gray colors. In addition to solids, there are the white-banded and tortoiseshell hamsters.

A cream satinized rex angora hamster. Photo by Michael Gilroy.

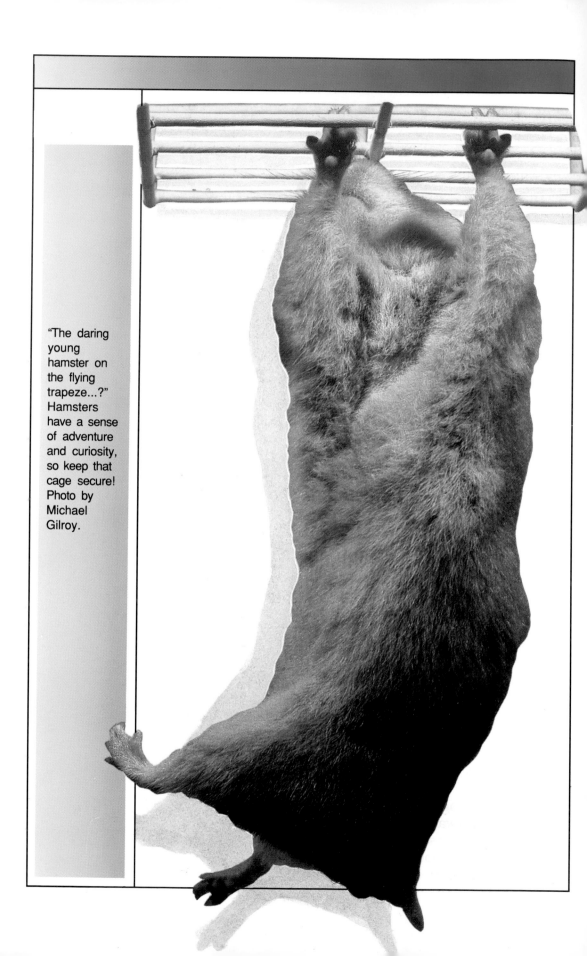

"The daring young hamster on the flying trapeze...?" Hamsters have a sense of adventure and curiosity, so keep that cage secure! Photo by Michael Gilroy.

VACATIONS AND YOUR HAMSTER

A hamster, unlike many other pet animals, can be left alone for several days, providing that you leave him with a good supply of dry food and enough fresh drinking water. It is possible to leave the hamster alone for a little longer, perhaps seven to ten days, but if you plan on doing this it would be advisable for you to get someone to at least look in on the animal every few days or so.

The important thing to remember is the water bottle—the water bottle has to be working and it has to be securely attached to the hamster's cage. To ensure that the hamster gets enough water you might even want to toss a piece of raw potato or an apple slice into his cage.

Remember to leave your thermostat set in the 65 to 72°F (18-22°C) range in winter. In the summer, put the hamster's cage in the coolest part of the house, especially during a summer heat wave.

Dwarf hamsters, originally from cooler climates and more northern Asian latitudes, can withstand cooler temperatures in the home.

For any type of hamster, make sure the cage is out of direct sunlight and not near any radiator, heat or air-conditioning vent.

What if you are going on vacation and will be gone for more than a few days, and for possibly a week or two? You have several choices. The best one is to find a good, reliable friend who you can count on, someone who knows something about animals and has taken care of animals before and is willing to put in the time and effort needed to take care of your pet.

Type up a list for your friend. This way you can be sure that you have mentioned everything, explained where everything is, and that your friend won't forget anything that is very important. Be sure to list such things as placement of the cage (you wouldn't, for example, want someone to make the mistake of putting the cage in the sunlight) in your home or theirs. It is

Hamsters appreciate variety in their snacks.

preferable to keep the hamster in your home, rather that moving him to your friend's home.

That list might also mention how often the hamster should be fed. You should buy everything before you leave. Make sure that whoever is watching

your hamster checks the water bottle to see that it isn't leaking and that your hamster is getting enough fresh drinking water.

Leave enough wood shavings for a change of litter and bedding. It is not advisable for the "hamster-sitter" to take the hamster out of the cage. There are several good reasons for this, one being that your hamster doesn't know the "sitter" as well as he knows you. Another reason is that it prevents the possibility, and headache, involved in a hamster escaping from his cage. And there is also the possibility that your hamster might nip his temporary guardian.

If your home is occupied in part by other animals, it might be a much better idea for you to bring the hamster, lock, stock and barrel, to your friend's house—providing, of course, that he or she doesn't have too many other animals to handle.

TRAVELING WITH YOUR HAMSTER

Then again, you *can*, if you so desire, bring your hamster along with you on your trip or vacation—to an extent, that is. For example, you would not want to take your hamster on a very long car trip. So, provided that your trip will be short, this should not

A cage of this size should serve only as temporary quarters or a travel cage and certainly not as permanent housing for the three animals occupying it here! Photo by Michael Gilroy.

be a problem. A hamster can be as easy to care for away from home as he can be in your home.

There are things for you to do to prepare him for the trip. Clean the hamster's cage a day or two before you are planning to leave. Make sure that there is enough clean bedding, not just for now but for the beginning of the trip as well. Make sure everything in the hamster's cage is secure so nothing can fall and hurt him. Take out anything heavy or loose that could fall on top of the hamster.

Bring along food, snacks, gnawing sticks, and an exercise wheel, along with a good supply of wood shavings for the cage. And don't forget to take the water bottle.

In the car, secure the cage and put it somewhere away from heating and/or air-conditioning vents in order to make the ride as comfortable as possible for the animal. Make sure that the cage is not put in direct sunlight or in the direct path of a strong window breeze.

If you need to make a stop, have someone stay in

A hamster "shoe-in" no doubt. Note the extremely sturdy construction, the better to withstand hamster teeth! Photo by Michael Gilroy.

the car with the hamster. And if your are alone and need to leave your car, park it in the shade and look in the back seat to be sure that everything is in place. In the summer, leave the car window open a little at the top to ensure that there is proper air circulation. Don't leave the hamster alone in the car for too long!

Make sure that, wherever you are staying, arrangements have been made in advance to accommodate you and your hamster. And wherever you are staying remember to put the cage where you would put it at home—out of direct sunlight and away from drafts.

Don't travel with a pregnant or nursing hamster. In fact, if at all possible, try to put off any travelling plans that you might have considered for this time. At this time,

Shorthaired gray hamster. Photo by Michael Gilroy.

The "hamster house," an ideal nest box and sleeping retreat. Photo by Michael Gilroy.

the pregnant or nursing hamster should be at home in familiar surroundings—and you should be there, too.

HISTORY OF THE PET HAMSTER

Professor I. Aharoni of the Department of Zoology at Hebrew University in Jerusalem is considered the father of the pet hamster. It was in 1930 that the professor was

out in the field near Aleppo, Syria, when he found a mother hamster and her litter. The professor took this "first family of pet hamsters" back

The animal that started it all—the Syrian, or golden, hamster, *Mesocricetus auratus*. Photo by Michael Gilroy.

Campbell's dwarf Russian hamster, *Phodopus sungoris campbelli.* Photo by Michael Gilroy.

to the university. The survivors were bred and became the source of every living golden hamster in the pet world today.

A year after the professor's discovery, several descendants of these hamsters were shipped to England, where they were sent to commercial breeders, a university and a zoo.

In 1938 some of these hamsters were sent to the United States Public Health Service Research Department in Carville, Louisiana, where they were used, at first, for medical research.

Research scientists there, no doubt, noticed that these hamsters had the qualifications to become good pets. They were cute, cuddly, friendly and interesting to watch, and it would not be long before they would catch on as a pet in the United States and in Europe.

This hamster—the Syrian, or golden, hamster, whose Latin name is *Mesocricetus auratus*— is the original pet hamster. The different color varieties—albino, black, beige and panda—are all variations of this animal.

For many years, the

Syrian hamster dominated the pet hamster scene until the fairly recent emergence of other types from other regions. These "new kids on the block"—the Chinese striped hamster (*Cricetulus griseus*) and the Djungarian or striped hairy-footed dwarf hamster (*Phodopus sungorus*)—are originally from northern Asia: Siberia, Mongolia and northern China.

The European, or field, hamster is much bigger than the pet hamsters. *Cricetus cricetus* is nine to ten inches long and does not make a good pet. He

Shorthaired gray satin hamster. Photo by Michael Gilroy.

A duo of shorthaired dark gray hamsters. Photo by Michael Gilroy.

can be found throughout Europe and in parts of Asia. The European hamster has a light brown coat with black underfur. He raids grain fields and gardens throughout Europe, digging intricate burrows underground and storing food there and staying there during the cold weather.

HAMSTERS IN THE WILD

You should never let your hamster get outdoors because of the dangers involved. However, before the hamster became a pet and before being transported overseas, the animal's several varieties

existed in several exotic and demanding environments. Golden hamsters, for example, come from the desert of the Middle East, where the temperature range is extreme and where the amount of water available is minimal.

To survive in the hot climate, the Syrian hamster sleeps during the day underground in a cool burrow. He goes out at night for food—seeds, insects and whatever desert greenery is available. You'll also find them wherever there is a grain field. Sometimes food is not available, and for

Dark gray satin angora hamster. Photo by Michael Gilroy.

this reason nature has endowed the hamster with those stretchable cheek pouches to carry home and store food.

Chinese and dwarf hamsters, from the northern regions of Asia, live in an almost entirely different world than their southern cousins. While the Syrian hamster's world is dominated by heat, the Chinese and dwarf hamsters'

environ ment is usually cold. Snow and cold temperatures send these hamsters deep underground for warmth. Because the summers are short and the winters are long, the Chinese and dwarf hamsters, like squirrels, gather food in the fall, which they store until the short summer begins.

A dwarf hamster "hanging in there" on a cage ladder. Wild hamsters won't encounter such a contraption in the natural habitat! **Opposite page:** A young male golden hamster strikes a pose in somewhat natural surroundings. Photos by Michael Gilroy.

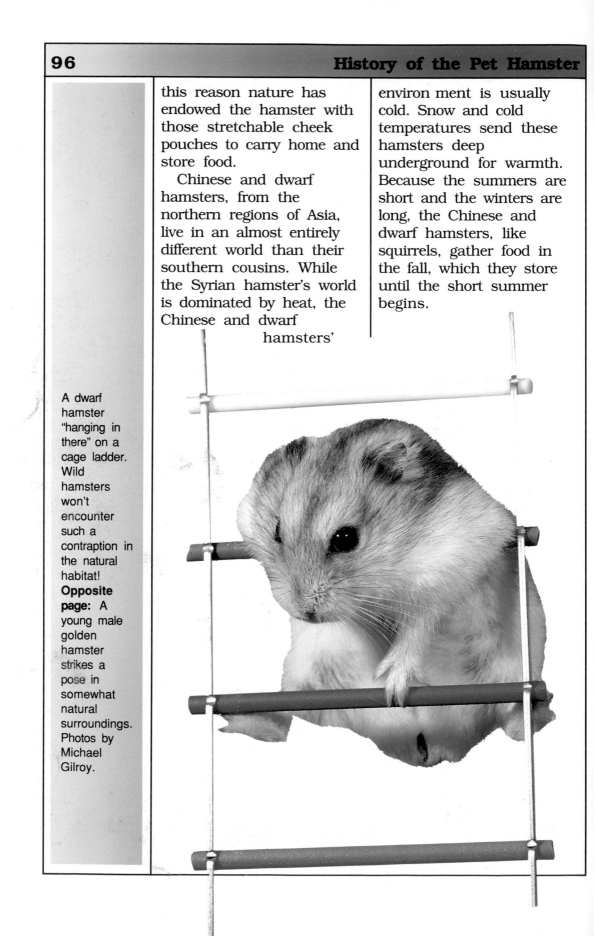

INDEX